Phonics Tales! ™

Mouse in My House!

by Violet Findley
Illustrated by Richard Torrey

SCHOLASTIC INC.

New York • Toronto • London • Auckland • Sydney
Mexico City • New Dehli • Hong Kong • Buenos Aires

Designed by Maria Lilja
ISBN-13: 978-0-439-88463-1 • ISBN-10: 0-439-88463-2
Copyright © 2006 by Scholastic Inc.
All rights reserved. Printed in the U.S.A.

First printing, November 2006

12 11 10 9 8 7 6 5 4 3 2 1   6 7 8 9 10 11/0

This is a story **about** the day I **found** a **mouse** in my **house**. It all started with a **loud** squeaking **sound**.

Phonics Fact

Sometimes the *ou* sound appears in the second syllable of a word, as in **around**. Be on the lookout for more *ou* words like this!

When I looked **around**, I saw a **mouse** on the **counter**.
"EEEEEEEEK!" I **shouted**. "Out of my **house**, Mouse!"

But that **mouse bounded** onto the **ground** and
bounced off my shoe. "**OUCH!**" I **shouted**.

Next, the **mouse** knocked over a five-**pound** bag of **flour**. Then, he scurried **about**, leaving **clouds** of **flour** all **around**!

"Out of my **house, Mouse!**" I **shouted**.
But that **mouse bounded** onto a **mountain**
of clothes and curled up on my best **blouse**!

"**Out** of my **house, Mouse!**" I **shouted**.
But the **mouse bounded** onto a **round** table.
He **pounced** on my **Sour** Gummy Worms and
ate **about** a **thousand**! (I **counted**.)

Then, that **lousy mouse bounded out** of the room. I was **outraged**! Where did he go? I **scouted around** for **hours**.

Well, I never **found** that **mouse**, so I plopped on the **couch** to **pout**.

And guess who was **lounging** beside me?
The **mouse**!

When I looked at the **mouse**, he was trembling. Why, that **mouse** was not **lousy** at all! He was just scared.

"I'm sorry I was a **grouch**," I said **loudly**.
Then that **mouse bounded** onto my hand.
"Squeak, squeak!" went his tiny **mouth**.

I am **proud** to say that the **mouse** and I are
now pals. In fact, he lives with me in my **house**.

And that **mouse** never bothers me an **ounce**. Except when he **devours** my **Sour** Gummy Worms!

OU Riddles

Listen to the riddles. Then match each riddle with the right *ou* word from the box.

Word Box

loud	sour	mouse	mouth	out
house	shout	found	hour	mountain

1 This tiny, furry animal loves cheese.

2 It is the opposite of *quiet*.

3 Lemons taste this way.

4 Another word for a *home*.

5 It is the same amount of time as 60 minutes.

6 It is the opposite of *lost*.

7 This means almost the same thing as *yell*.

8 You use this part of your body to eat and talk.

9 It is the opposite of *in*.

10 This is the word for a *very, very tall hill*.

OU Cheer

Hooray for *o-u*, the best pair around!

Let's holler *o-u* words all over town!

There's **house** and **mouse** and **scout** and **found**.

There's **out** and **pout** and **round** and **ground**.

There's **count** and **south** and **mouth** and **cloud**.

There's **bounce** and **ounce** and **trout** and **proud**.

O-u, o-u, give a great cheer,

For the **loudest sound** you ever will hear!

Make a list of other *ou* words. Then use them in your cheer.